To the memory of my father, Gordon Minor,
a man of the Great Outdoors—W. M.

SIERRA

By Diane Siebert ◆ Paintings by Wendell Minor

HarperCollins*Publishers*

I am the mountain,
Tall and grand.
And like a sentinel I stand.

Surrounding me, my sisters rise
With watchful peaks that pierce the skies;
From north to south we form a chain
Dividing desert, field, and plain.

I am the mountain.
Come and know
Of how, ten million years ago,
Great forces, moving plates of earth,
Brought, to an ancient land, rebirth;
Of how this planet's faulted crust
Was shifted, lifted, tilted, thrust
Toward the sky in waves of change
To form a newborn mountain range.

I am the mountain,
Young, yet old.
I've stood, and watching time unfold,
Have known the age of ice and snow
And felt the glaciers come and go.
They moved with every melt and freeze;
They shattered boulders, leveled trees,
And carved, upon my granite rocks,
The terraced walls of slabs and blocks
That trace each path, each downward course,
Where through the years, with crushing force,
The glaciers sculpted deep ravines
And polished rocks to glossy sheens.

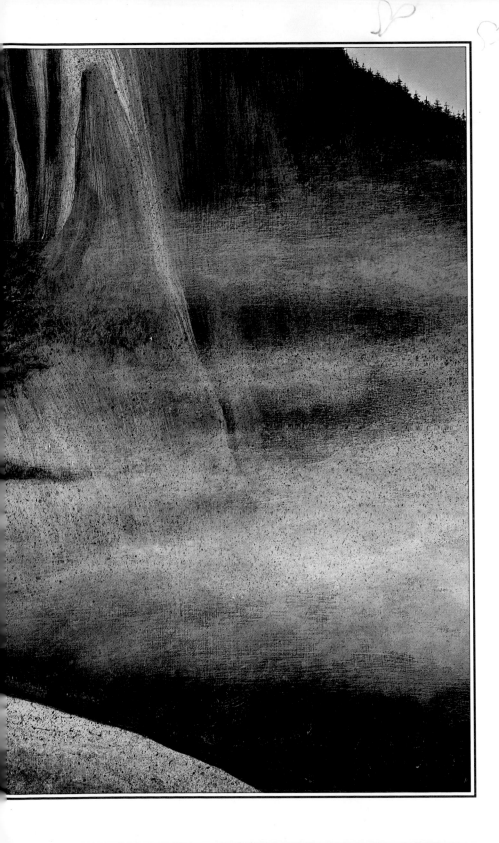

At last this era, long and cold,
Began to lose its frigid hold
When, matched against a warming sun,
Its final glacier, ton by ton,
Retreated, melting, making way
For what I have become today:

A place of strength and lofty height;
Of shadows shot with shafts of light;
Where meadows nestle in between
The arms of forests, cool and green;
Where, out of clefted granite walls,
Spill silver, snow-fed waterfalls.

Here stand the pines, so straight and tall,
Whose needles, dry and dying, fall
Upon my sides to slowly form
A natural blanket, soft and warm;
Their graceful, swaying branches sing
In gentle breezes, whispering
To junipers, all gnarled and low,
That here, in stubborn splendor, grow.

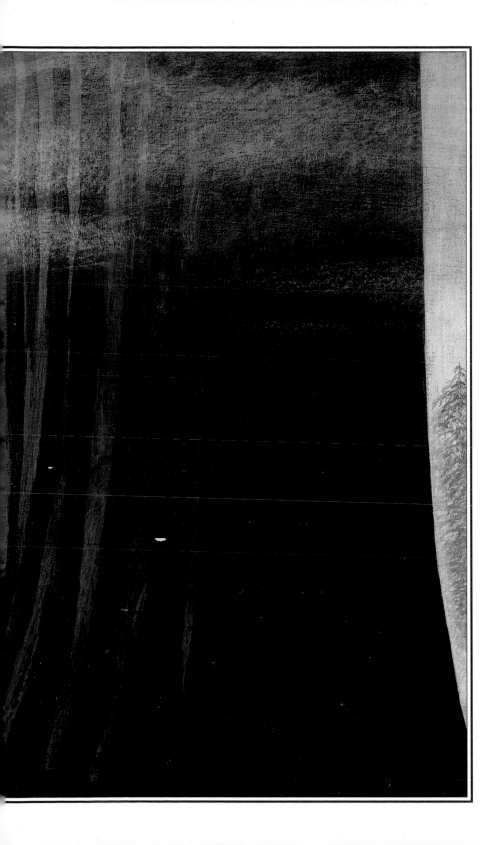

And on my western slope I hold
My great sequoias, tall and old;
They've watched three thousand years go by,
And, in their endless quest for sky,
This grove of giants slowly grew
With songs of green on silent blue.

I am the mountain.
In each breath
I feel the pull of life and death
As untamed birds and beasts obey
The laws of predator and prey.

On me, the hunted ones reside,
Sustained by foods my plants provide:

I keep the pikas, small and shy,
That spread their gathered grass to dry.

I shelter rodents. In my trees
Live pinecone-loving chickarees,
While tunnels, crevices, and holes
Hold marmots, ground squirrels,
chipmunks, voles.

I cradle herds of graceful deer
That drink from waters cold and clear;
I know each buck with antlers spread
Above his proud, uplifted head.
I know each doe, each spotted fawn,
In sunshine seen, in shadows, gone.

I know these creatures, every one.
They, to survive, must hide or run;
As food for those that stalk and chase,
Within life's chain, they have a place.

Then, too, the predators are mine,
Each woven into earth's design.
I feel them as they wake and rise;
I see the hunger in their eyes.

These are the coyotes, swift and lean;
The bobcats, shadowy, unseen;
The martens in their tree-branch trails;
The masked raccoons with long, ringed tails;
The mountain lions and big black bears
That live within my rocky lairs;
The owls that prowl the skies at night;
The hawks and eagles, free in flight.

I know them all. I understand.
They keep the balance on the land.
They take the old, the sick, the weak;
And as they move, their actions speak
In tones untouched by right or wrong:
     We hunt to live.
     We, too, belong.

I am the mountain.
        From the sea
Come constant winds to conquer me—
Pacific winds that touch my face
And bring the storms whose clouds embrace
My rugged shoulders, strong and wide;
And in their path, I cannot hide.

And though I have the strength of youth,
I sense each change and know the truth:
By wind and weather, day by day,
I will, in time, be worn away;
For mountains live, and mountains die.
As ages pass, so, too, will I.

But while my cloak of life exists,
I'll cherish winds and storms and mists,
For in them, precious gifts are found
As currents carry scent and sound;
As every gust and playful breeze
Helps sow the seeds of parent trees;
As silver drops and soft white flakes
Fill laughing streams and alpine lakes;
As lightning fires, hot and bright,
Thin undergrowth, allowing light
To reach the fresh, cleared soil below
So roots can spread and trees can grow.

I am the mountain,
Tall and grand,
And like a sentinel I stand.
Yet I, in nature's wonders draped,
Now see this mantle being shaped
By something new—a force so real
That every part of me can feel
Its actions changing nature's plan.
Its numbers grow. Its name is MAN.
And what my course of life will be
Depends on how man cares for me.

I am the mountain,
Tall and grand.
And like a sentinel I stand.

DIANE SIEBERT and her husband have traveled extensively through much of the United States. Ms. Siebert has spent a great deal of time camping, hiking, and running in the Sierra Nevada. She and her husband now live in central Oregon with their dogs, pet rats, and the deer, coyotes, and various other wildlife that visit on a daily basis. Her love for the earth is a continuing source of inspiration for her writing. Ms. Siebert is the author of five other picture books: TRAIN SONG, HEARTLAND, MOJAVE, TRUCK SONG, and PLANE SONG.

WENDELL MINOR was born in Aurora, Illinois, and was graduated from the Ringling School of Art and Design in Sarasota, Florida. Well known in the publishing industry for the paintings he has done for the jackets of many best-selling novels, he is the recipient of over two hundred professional awards. Before beginning work on the paintings for SIERRA, Mr. Minor hiked the High Sierra Loop in Yosemite National Park. Mr. Minor is the illustrator of HEARTLAND and MOJAVE by Diane Siebert; THE SEASHORE BOOK by Charlotte Zolotow; and JULIE, EVERGLADES, and THE MOON OF THE OWLS by Jean Craighead George.

Sierra. Text copyright © 1991 by Diane Siebert. Illustrations copyright © 1991 by Wendell Minor. Printed in the U.S.A. All rights reserved. Typography by Al Cetta. Library of Congress Cataloging-in-Publication Data. Siebert, Diane. Sierra / Diane Siebert ; paintings by Wendell Minor. p. cm. Summary: One of the Sierra Nevada mountains speaks of the beauty and timelessness of herself and her sister peaks. ISBN 0-06-021639-5. — ISBN 0-06-021640-9 (lib bdg.). — ISBN 0-06-443441-9 (pbk.) [Sierra Nevada Mountains (California and Nevada)—Fiction. 2. Stories in rhyme.] I. Minor, Wendell, ill. II. Title. PZ8.3.S5725Si 1991 90-30522 [E]—dc20 CIP AC The art in this book is acrylic on gessoed Masonite panels.